Praise for Money LifeHacks

*The real American Dream is not just to get
a great salary, work for 35 years and retire.
Rather, it's to live a life of purpose and meaning,
using money as a tool but also seeking physical,
emotional, spiritual, and relational abundance.
Money LifeHacks, a humorous and engaging book,
will move you from "I wish" to "I will".*

— Dan Miller,
New York Times best-selling author,
48 Days to the Work You Love

**Man Upstairs LifeHacks™
presents:**

MONEY
LIFEHACKS

A 60-Minute Beginner's Guide to
Rethinking Your Personal Finances

Gabriel Aviles

TABLE OF CONTENTS

FOREWORD

Life can be complicated. Regardless of our sex, age, race, geography, or income, we humans face money, relationship, health, and other complex issues on a consistent basis. This can leave us exhausted and even hopeless.

Adding to the complexity of life is what seems to be an endless array of potential solutions to these problems. We can google anything we might need or find a do-it-yourself video on YouTube, or even post something on Facebook, asking our hundreds of friends for advice.

Although help is available from multiple sources, people from all walks of life in this postmodern age still turn to the all-knowing Man Upstairs (that is, God) and the Good Book (aka the Bible) to find the best answers to both difficult and everyday questions. I'm one of those guys.

WHY THE BIBLE?

You're probably familiar with God, or at least some aspect of God, and you may have even skimmed through a Bible once or twice. Still, you may wonder why I believe we can draw wisdom from this timeless book.

The reason is simple. More than a collection of ancient writings, the Bible is a collection of sixty-six smaller books that were written by humans but inspired by the Man Upstairs. Even though each author's unique personality and experiences shine through their work, I believe God guided these authors to communicate exactly what He wanted to say through these letters, historical records, and books of wisdom.

For 2000 years this wisdom has guided people and continues to do so today. Think of the Bible as our very own "owner's manual," written by the Man Upstairs who created us.

WHERE DO I START?

Having an owner's manual and using it effectively, however, are two separate things. Maybe you want to know what your Owner's Manual has to say about a certain issue or problem, but you don't know where to begin. The Bible's size alone can be intimidating. And while some Bibles contain concordances, dictionaries, maps, and other resources, we still may not be sure if we should be starting in Genesis, Revelation, or somewhere in between.

I'M KIND OF BUSY

Besides not knowing where to start, time is often a hindrance when it comes to looking for answers in the Bible. The demands of our home, careers, and other obligations leave us little room for much else.

Even if we are able to find the time to look at the "Good Book," and can eventually find what we're looking for, the Bible can sometimes be difficult to understand. After all, it was written a long time ago in a very different world by a diverse group of authors writing in their individual styles. Even modern translations can sometimes leave us scratching our heads a bit (kind of like when I had to read the oldest surviving Old English poem, "Beowulf," in high school).

THIS SERIES IS FOR YOU

If any of this sounds familiar, the Man Upstairs LifeHacks book series is a great starting point. Although not meant to exhaust each topic, each book in the series summarizes what the Good Book says about important topics like money, work, and life. We do it in entertaining, easy-to-understand language, with the goal of cutting to the chase and letting you get on with your life.

STILL NOT SURE?

I understand you may not believe the same things I believe about the Bible. You may wonder if the Bible is still relevant today. You may wonder if God truly spoke through these writers. You may wonder if God even exists at all.

Those are good questions, and you're certainly not on your own. Many feel the same way.

While this series may not answer all of your questions, I invite you to take this short journey with me. You never know. You may actually find some practical solutions to your everyday problems anyway.

INTRODUCTION

Whenever I speak to groups of people — even if I have been briefed ahead of time on who will be present — the first thing I do is poll the audience. Depending on the setting, I'm interested in knowing if they've heard me speak before, where they're from, and why they decided to show up. I find this exercise helpful not only as a warm-up, but also as a way to adjust and better tailor my message, if I need to.

So even though I can't physically see you, I have to ask. What drew you to this book? Why are you choosing to read it?

Maybe your finances are in order, but you're reading this because you devour books, magazines, blogs, radio shows, podcasts, and anything else related to money. You read and know so much about personal finances that you're even doubtful that there will be anything here you don't already know (but you're reading it just in case).

On the other hand, maybe you live with your parents because you can't afford your own place. You're flat broke and thinking about pawning that big screen television you purchased with your credit card. You are desperately looking for answers and are hoping this book will provide them.

Maybe you're not quite sure why you're reading, but something about the title or cover intrigued you. You have a sense of the importance of having your personal finances in order, although you don't particularly feel like you have any major issues. You feel good about your money habits and simply want to make sure you stay on track.

Then again, maybe you were "coerced" by a well-meaning family member or friend and it's just easier to read it than to say no.

Whatever the reason, I'm glad you're here!

GRADE SCHOOL HUSTLING

I was born in Chile, lived in New York City during first grade, and then moved to the small town of Collegedale, Tennessee, where I lived until the age of twenty.

It was early on in that small town of less than 5,000 that I began to find little ways to make cash. As a grade-schooler, I made money going from house to house selling greeting cards from a catalog, helping my neighbor with light construction duties, selling Spanish lessons to a few takers in my fifth grade class, and becoming an unofficial reseller of Oatmeal Crème Pies and other Little Debbie Snack Cakes at school (long story).

MONEY BELIEFS

What I didn't realize back then is that I already had my own beliefs about money. The time I spent looking for work and creating new ideas to generate revenue showcased my belief in money being something desirable. The way I spent that money on Matchbox cars or a new Walkman (remember those?) displayed my propensity to spend it on fun instead of saving it for the future was also indicative of my money beliefs.

What about you? What deep-seated beliefs and mind-sets do you have about money?

Do you love money and continually look for ways to earn more? If so, what drives this desire? What would happen if you truly had all of the money you wished for?

On the other hand, does the mere mention of money cause you stress? Maybe you've never felt like you've had enough and/or fear not having enough in the future.

Or maybe you even fear having too much? You have a deep-seated belief that money is evil and a destructive force.

WHY BOTHER?

Whether you have all you need or are barely surviving financially, reconsidering your current thinking about your personal finances is a good exercise. Looking beyond the mechanics of budgeting, spending, and saving can be eye opening, since the way we think about money has a significant impact on us. These money mind-sets have the potential to drive behavior that either sets us on the course for lifelong success or derails us from our life's purpose.

Mahatma Gandhi, the great leader of the Indian independence movement of the early twentieth century, is quoted as saying:

> *"Your beliefs become your thoughts, Your thoughts become your words, Your words become your actions, Your actions become your habits, Your habits become your values, Your values become your destiny."*

While he wasn't specifically talking about money, our beliefs about our cash colors all aspects of our lives. They help to determine what we do for a living, where we live, how we spend our time, where we go on vacation, when we retire, and so much more. The way we think about money today has a long-term impact, not only for us but for our families, both present and future. Our beliefs about money turn into actions that turn into habits, that turn into values, that do, in fact, impact our own destinies as well as the destinies of those in generations to come!

WHAT'S AHEAD

While beliefs about money abound, this book highlights six key money concepts, laid out by God and found in the Bible. God has provided a lot more advice on this topic than you may think. In fact, when Jesus spoke to people, he focused more on the subject of money than just about any other topic.

As a whole, the Bible contains over one hundred verses in both the Old and New Testaments that refer in some way to the acquisition and use of money. Some of these verses provide direct advice on how to use — or not use — it. Some warn against the consequences of financial dishonesty or ignorance. Others still use this subject of as a means of teaching deeper, universal truths.

Before continuing, I want to let you in on a secret. I'm just a regular person like you! Sure, I have a certification in Dave Ramsey's Financial Coach Master Series, and I've studied financial, leadership, and coaching topics. I'm working toward completion of a course with business guru Dan Miller too. But at the end of the day, I'm a guy with a wife and three small children, trying to share a bit of what I've learned by digging into the Good Book. And yes, I truly believe that grabbing hold of these simple money attitudes will set you up for lifelong success!

Chapter 1

So Happy Together

I can't see me loving nobody but you for all my life.
When you're with me, baby, the skies'll be blue for all
my life.

— from the song "Happy Together"
by Gary Bonner and Alan Gordon,
recorded by the Turtles

In spite of sporting a not-so-attractive peach fuzz mustache, being subpar in the fashion department, and having enough athletic ability to consistently place me in the "B" league intramural sports teams, it still happened. I was still able to convince a spirited, cute redhead to "go with me" my freshman year in high school.

Those were good times, going to classes together, talking, laughing, and getting in trouble for talking and laughing. Like any couple that were truly in love, we also had "our" songs ("Heaven In Your Eyes" by Loverboy and "Will You Still Love Me" by Chicago).

As the school year progressed, we started liking each other more and, eventually, I believed that we would be so "happy together." I wanted to get married and couldn't imagine being happy any other way. I knew that this relationship was surely the key to lifelong happiness. Even our school receptionist shared this vision and started calling us Mr. and Mrs. Aviles.

THE LETDOWN

As it turned out, our receptionist jumped the gun. Due to some unfortunate circumstances (long story), our "lifelong romance" ended sometime in our sophomore year. Yes, the dream was over. Romance had let me down. Happiness had eluded me.

Just as I had equated happiness with romance, some of us hang our hopes for happiness on money. We expect it to make us happy. We expect it to bring us happiness that lasts. We expect that having more of it will bring deeper levels of euphoria, but is that really the case?

GROSS NATIONAL HAPPINESS

The link between money and happiness has been studied for decades. In one study, researchers actually set out to determine a country's "Gross National Happiness" quotient based on its wealth. In this landmark 1974 University of Southern California study, economist and professor Richard Easterlin found that two nations with a large disparity between their gross national products had essentially the same amount of gross national happiness. In other words, the richest and poorest nations were equally happy — or unhappy. This notion was reaffirmed in a similar Easterlin study in 2010, when he studied data from thirty-seven countries.

Other number crunchers disagree, however, saying Professor Easterlin didn't ask the right questions. In 2008, Researchers Betsey Stevenson and Justin Wolfers from the University of Pennsylvania published a paper called, "Economic Growth and Subjective Well-Being," showing that wealthier people are generally more satisfied with life than their poorer counterparts. However, due to the law of diminishing returns, each additional dollar earned tends to "buy" less happiness than the dollar before it.

While the results of these two studies differ somewhat, I think we can surmise from both that once the basics of food, shelter, and clothing are covered, having more money doesn't necessarily increase happiness.

WISH LIST

This theory has also proven to be true in my own life. My first job in the music business was an assistant position at a record label in Nashville. I loved my work and was happy to be bringing home $18,000 in annual salary. I had enough to cover my basics, as well as a little extra to eat out or take a trip to the beach.

The interesting thing, however, is that even though my salary has consistently increased over the years, something I desired and pursued, I can't necessarily say that the happiness quotient has risen commensurate with salary increases.

I'm not saying that my level of happiness has decreased over the years; I typically wake up on the right side of the bed (literally) and I'm as happy today as I was when I was making $8.65/hour. But wouldn't it seem obvious that I would be even happier now, making more money?

Don't get me wrong. Making more money is certainly helpful, especially now that I'm a husband and father of three active children. It would be tough for us to afford diapers, Cub Scouts, or ballet lessons, while still having my wife stay home and homeschool on an $18,000 salary. So though I'm thankful to have more to cover what my family needs, I certainly have my wish list today, as I did when I made much less, of potential purchases that would make our lives simpler and/or more enjoyable. But will obtaining these things really make our family happier or will crossing off these items from our list simply open up space for us to add more items to our wish list?

ONE WISH

To see what the Bible says about money and happiness, let's go straight to the story of the richest and wisest man in the Bible, King Solomon (1 Kings 2–11). He built a very large temple, a huge palace for himself, and the wall around Jerusalem. He built cities. He had a thousand women in his harem, including seven hundred wives of royal birth and three hundred additional mistresses.

The way Solomon became so wise is interesting. Early in his kingship, God appeared to him during the night. He said to Solomon, "Ask for whatever you want me to give you." A lot of us would have gone for the money, but Solomon asked God for wisdom to better lead the Israelites instead. God was so pleased with Solomon's selfless wish that, He gave the king both wisdom and riches!

*Since you have asked for this and not for long
life or wealth for yourself, nor have asked for the
death of your enemies but for discernment in
administering justice, I will do what you have
asked. I will give you a wise and discerning heart,
so that there will never have been anyone like you,
nor will there ever be. Moreover, I will give you
what you have not asked for — both wealth and
honor — so that in your lifetime you will have no
equal among kings. (1 Kings 3:11–13)*

HAPPIEST MAN ALIVE

Now that Solomon had riches (and wisdom and fame), did
this make him Mr. Happy? Was he the most content, most
satisfied man alive?

Not so much. The book of Proverbs is packed with
Solomon's observations about the dangers of money.
The book of Ecclesiastes, a jaded autobiography of his
accomplishments, expresses how empty life can be even for
the very rich and powerful.

*I have seen a grievous evil under the sun:
wealth hoarded to the harm of its owners,
or wealth lost through some misfortune,
so that when they have children
there is nothing left for them to inherit.
Everyone comes naked from their mother's womb,*

and as everyone comes, so they depart.
They take nothing from their toil
that they can carry in their hands."

(Ecclesiastes 5:13–15)

No, money did not turn Solomon into the happiest man alive. If you follow his life story through to the end, you'll find that Solomon allowed his lavish lifestyle to cloud his judgment. He made some pretty bad decisions, including some that led to the once-unified Israel splitting into two separate kingdoms. Things pretty much went downhill fast from there.

GREAT EXPECTATIONS

While having great wealth didn't result in happiness for Solomon, it doesn't mean that you and I should not have it or even pursue it. After all, we need money or wealth to purchase or barter for what we need to survive. We can also use currency to provide us with nice things and experiences that bring us a certain level of satisfaction and enjoyment.

The key, however, is to not place such great expectations on money. Money, unfortunately, is not up to the challenge. There's only so much that currency can do for us. There's only so much happiness that money can buy.

Money LifeHack #1

Money ≠ Happiness

STOP and THINK

1. Is it hard for you to separate money and happiness?

2. Has this belief caused you anxiety?

3. What are other things in your life that are more important than money?

Chapter 2

For the Love of Money

For the love of money, people will steal from their mother.
For the love of money, people will rob their own brother.

— *from the song "For the Love of Money" by Kenneth Gamble, Leon Huff, and Anthony Jackson, performed by the O'Jays*

Yes, I made her cry. The first (and only) time my wife and I played the board game Monopoly, the waterworks started. I wasn't trying to make the tears roll, of course, but apparently the nature of the game and my love of winning this game of skill, talent, and luck (okay, mostly luck) brought out what she would say is an ugly side of me.

In case you have not played this game of economic domination, players move around the game board by buying up properties, adding homes and hotels along the way. If someone lands on another's property, the unfortunate soul must pay rent, determined by a base price, along with the number of houses on the property (or hotel). The goal of the game is to drive others to bankruptcy. Sounds romantic, doesn't it?

Therein lies the problem. Apparently, I take phrases like economic domination and bankruptcy too seriously, even when I play against my wife. While I certainly don't intend to be mean, she sees certain aspects of my personality that she's not used to seeing. I'm not sure I'm to blame though. After all, this "Fast-Dealing Property Trading Game" is meant to be won, right? It makes sense to me, although my wife doesn't appreciate paying me large sums of fake money. This incident led me to conclude that Monopoly is not quite the at-home date night aphrodisiac I had it hoped it would be.

INNOCENT MAN

Believe it or not, I really wasn't doing anything wrong while I was playing Monopoly, other than possibly getting a bit too excited about crushing my opponent.

I was playing by the rules and raking in the winnings accordingly.

That's not always the case, however, in the real world. Sometimes those who are "raking it in" turn into other people. People their loved ones don't recognize. An otherwise upright citizen, given the right opportunity to make money, can let that quest turn into an obsession. This obsession can cloud their judgment and ability to make moral choices, often leaving a path of destruction.

LUXURY CARS and FIFTY DOLLARS

This link between moral behavior and money was studied by social psychologist Paul Piff from the University of California–Berkeley. He has specifically researched how social hierarchy, inequality, and emotions shape relations between individuals and groups.

In one experiment, published in the March 13, 2012, issue of *Proceedings of the National Academy of Sciences*, Piff found that those who drive BMWs, Mercedes, Porsches, and other luxury cars are less likely to stop for pedestrians at crosswalks. He also found that those with higher means are four times more likely to cheat in a card game when there's fifty dollars on the line.

PARKER BROTHERS
REAL ESTATE TRADING GAME

Interestingly enough, Piff also experimented with a game of — you guessed it — Monopoly. In this experiment, one person started out with more money than the other. It turns out that when participants who were given more money won the game, they didn't acknowledge being given a leg up, insisting, instead, they'd won fair and square.

These results from Piff's numerous studies, along with studies by Harvard University and the University of Utah (*New York Times*, 13 June 2013, "How Money Affects Morality" by Eduardo Porter) indicate that the wealthy have lower ethical standards than those with less. In other words, Piff makes the case that money actually does erode ones morals.

Many of us, of course, would call Piff "Captain Obvious." Did he really need to go through all of that to come this conclusion? Money has started wars, broken homes, and corrupted society. Isn't it obvious that money is evil or, as the Bible says, the root of all evil?

RICHES TO RAGS

If being rich is evil, is living in rags the way to be a good person? Is a vow of poverty the best way to maintain our integrity and be upright citizens?

Paul Piff's findings certainly line up with the thinking of those of us who grew up in the '80s (otherwise known as the Decade of Excess). While we secretly envied lifestyles portrayed in television shows like *Miami Vice* (starring the then fashion-forward Don Johnson) and songs like Dire Straits' "Money For Nothing," deep down, something told us that having loads of money was somehow wrong.

Even what I knew then of the Bible confirmed the notion that being wealthy was wrong. After all, Jesus, in the book of Matthew, tells a rich young man that it's easier for a camel to pass through the eye of the needle than for a rich man to get into heaven.

But what does the Bible really say?

RICH YOUNG MAN

Let's first examine the passage I referenced above, in Matthew 19:24. This verse is found within the story of a rich young man who asked Jesus how he could live eternally. Jesus told him that he should keep the commandments; the young man said he had always done that. Jesus went on to tell him to sell his possessions and give to the poor, at which point the young man became sad because he was unwilling to do so.

Jesus used this example to show his followers that it is difficult for a rich man to enter heaven. In fact, it's harder than a camel passing through the eye of a needle, he told them (Matthew 19:24).

EYE OF A NEEDLE?

If we take this verse literally and look at it in isolation, we can take it a step further than Jesus did. While he's suggesting it's difficult, we could safely say it's an impossibility.

But what does Jesus really mean by using the "eye of the needle" analogy? Was he really saying that rich people can't get into heaven?

Over the centuries, some have claimed that Jerusalem had a gate that opened after the main one closed, called "eye of the needle." A camel could only get through this gate if its baggage was removed, and it stooped down and scooted itself through.

Others sources reference small gates, low-arched doors, or otherwise small entrances where the same would have to occur. The camel would be able to make it through; it would just be a tedious process.

Whether the "eye of the needle" was an actual gate or not, let me suggest to you that Jesus, being a great storyteller, may have simply been using hyperbole or an exaggerated statement. He was using the phrase to prove a point, just as he did when he referenced a "plank" in one's eye (Matthew 7:3–5) or swallowing a camel (Matthew 23:24). In other words, even though he was saying that it might be tough for a rich man to enter heaven, he wasn't necessarily saying it's impossible.

In fact, if we look a few verses down, within the same setting (Matthew 19:26), Jesus goes on to clearly state that things that seem impossible to man are actually possible through God. In other words, even a rich man has the possibility of knowing God and living eternally.

NOT THE WHOLE STORY

Although what we've read so far from the Bible about money and evil is true, it's not the whole story. The Bible has more to say about money and evil in the New Testament book of 1 Timothy:

> *For the love of money is a root of all kinds of evil.*
> *(1 Timothy 6:10)*

If we read this one too fast, we might miss the importance of the word love. The verse is not saying that money is the root of all kinds of evil. It's actually saying that the love of money is the root of all evil. In the original Greek (the language of the New Testament), this use of the word love, is translated as "avarice" or "greed."

In other words, having money is not wrong. Having an abundance of wealth is not wrong. In fact, the Bible itself has examples of real people like Job, Abraham, and David who were wealthy, yet are still celebrated in the Bible as men who loved God and served him.

What the Bible warns us about is having an intense and excessive desire to accumulate money. Being consumed with the pursuit of wealth is what the Bible calls the "root of all kinds of evil."

I WANT TO KNOW WHAT LOVE IS

But how do we know when we've crossed the line from "like" to "love"? How do we know when we've taken our affection for money too far?

Asking ourselves a few questions may help. For example, is our pursuit of money affecting our relationships? Do we work so hard to accumulate wealth that we don't take the time to love the ones closest to us?

Is our health being affected? Are we losing sleep, thinking about how to make more money? Is our stress level so high that we're weakening our immune system and setting ourselves up for sickness?

What about our integrity? Are we willing to compromise our character and reputation for the right price?

These are good starter questions for us to determine whether we're in danger of loving money too much.

LET'S MAKE MONEY!

So let's go ahead! Let's make it, use it, enjoy it, and make more of it! Money. Let's create as much wealth as our God-given abilities and imagination will allow. Let's just remember to not let it overtake our lives. Let's not allow the love of money to become more important than the things that really matter in life.

Money LifeHack #2

Money is not evil

STOP and THINK

1. Do you have a hard time believing that money is not evil?

2. How has your view of money, whether good or evil, affected your personal finances?

3. How can your wealth be used for good?

Chapter 3

My Prerogative

I spent half my money on gambling, alcohol, and wild women. The other half I wasted.

— W. C. Fields (twentieth-century American juggler, comedian, actor, writer)

The beauty of my parents not believing in giving us allowances was that it drove me to be industrious at an early age. Earlier in the book, I shared with you my grade school work résumé as a door-to-door greeting card salesman, construction site assistant, Spanish tutor, and snack cake reseller. Paychecks during my high school and college years were earned as a janitor, Taco Bell drive-through king, mobile DJ, cutlery door-to-door salesman, and leads generator for Matchmaker video-dating service (yet another long story).

Although I enjoyed most of my forays into these various vocational endeavors, what I loved most was having my own money and being able to call the shots on how to spend it!

Even when I moved out during the latter part of my college years and became responsible for my own rent and bills, I still enjoyed earning my own money, paying my own bills, and deciding what to do with the little bit of my money that remained. Although I was unlikely to follow W. C. Field's advice, I loved the fact that it was my prerogative to do what I wanted to do with my loot.

I'm guessing you're no different. You have that same level of satisfaction when you're able to make your own financial decision and spend your money your way.

SELF-MADE

Since the nineteenth century, the term *self-made* has been used to describe people who were not born with a silver spoon in their mouths, but became individuals of influence and wealth regardless. Men like Benjamin Franklin, Abraham Lincoln, and Andrew Carnegie are still celebrated for "pulling themselves up by their own bootstraps" and making their mark.

In the twenty-first century, people like Bill Gates, Oprah Winfrey, and Richard Branson are also celebrated as self-made men and women. Our culture exalts these entrepreneurs for rising to greatness in spite of their roots.

Unless you've been given substantial amounts of money, property, or things by family, through an inheritance, or have won the lottery, most of us would also consider ourselves self-made. We've worked hard to achieve a certain level of financial success.

But is there really such a thing as a self-made man or woman? While I agree that Benjamin Franklin, Bill Gates, and the others mentioned above deserve recognition, can we truly call them self-made? Is there really such a thing as an army of one?

THE GIFT

The Old Testament book of Deuteronomy gives us some insight into this question. In chapter 8, we find God reminding Israel of a few things, including how he fed them in the desert with white fluffy bread called manna, protected them from poisonous snakes and scorpions, and gave them water from a rock.

In verses 17 and 18, he also makes it clear that although they used their strength and hands to produce their wealth, it wasn't all of their doing.

> You may say to yourself, "My power and the strength of my hands have produced this wealth for me." But remember the Lord your God, for it is he who gives you the ability to produce wealth.

In other words, God is the one who actually makes our wealth accumulation possible. He gives us health, intellect, talents, opportunities, relationships and anything else we might need to earn income.

Solomon, the wealthy and wise one, has a similar take on wealth. While he recognizes hard work in Ecclesiastes 5 ("toilsome labor"), he goes on to say that wealth and possessions are a gift from God. God allows the circumstances to unfold that provide us the opportunity to generate wealth.

WHITE ELEPHANT

If you've never been part of a Christmas "white elephant" gift exchange, you've missed out. There are variations of the game, but typically the inexpensive gifts are either funny, useless, tacky, or all of the above.

Another hallmark of the gift exchange, which typically takes place in a party setting, is that the gift-giver may not give the present that he or she brought to the party much thought. Sure, there are overachievers who do, in fact, spend weeks planning for the perfect present, but as a rule, this is not the case. Partygoers will look around the house or choose to regift something from a previous exchange.

Along with not giving the gift much thought, the gift-giver typically doesn't consider if the gift-recipient will like the gift or find it useful. The gift is mostly given to gain entrance into the festivities and to garner a good laugh when the present is opened.

That's not the way it is with God, though. The gifts he gives us, including money and the ability to make it, are not given to us flippantly. The power to make money is given to us with a purpose ... even expectation.

It's similar to when I give my kids presents. While it's "their" trampoline, I expect them to use the toy that cost us hundreds of dollars and take care of it.

SEVENTY-FIVE POUND BAG OF MONEY

In Matthew, chapter 25, verses 14 through 30, we find Jesus telling a group of his followers gathered at the

Mount of Olives about a man who was about to take a trip. Before leaving, he called his servants together to entrust some money to them. The first servant received five talents, the second got two talents, and the third servant one talent.

A talent is a unit of weight and value that was used by various ancient cultures. While different sources vary in their opinion of the actual weight and value of a talent during the time Jesus lived, most agree that a talent was a respectable amount of money.

Verse 19 tells us that "after a long time," the master of the servants returned and asked each of the servants what they had done with his money. It turns out that the servant who had been given five talents now had another five and the servant who had been given two talents had also doubled what he had been given.

The Bible is not clear on how they both doubled their master's money, but it's clear they took action. Maybe they started a business, invested in someone else's business, or sold items on Ebay. We don't know for sure, but we know that they doubled the investment and that their master was very pleased. In fact, he told them both, "well done" and called them good and faithful servants.

THE HIDER

The third servant, however, did not have such a good report. No, he didn't lose any money, but he didn't make any either. He still had the same talent that he was given before his master's journey.

When the master asked him for an explanation, the last servant told his master that he dug a hole and buried his talent because he was afraid of losing it.

The master, of course, was not very happy with the hider. In fact, the master actually called the hider servant "wicked" and "slothful."

WORD OF THE DAY

The story above clearly exemplifies the concept of "stewardship." The word steward, according to the Merriam-Webster dictionary, is "someone who protects or is responsible for money, property, etc.," or "a person whose job is to manage the land and property of another person."

For purposes of our discussion, we can say that God, like the master in the biblical example, expects us to be good stewards of our personal finances. He wants us to handle our financial affairs in a way that recognizes that this money is his. He's simply allowing us the opportunity to work hand-in-hand with him on how to spend, save, and invest it.

It's like managing expenses at work. Yes, I'm free to spend money to accomplish my job, but there is an expectation on how it's spent. I'm expected to spend it wisely. After all, it's not my money; I'm just managing or stewarding it on behalf of my employer.

MYTH BUSTERS

We've now busted a couple of myths. First of all, none of us are truly self-made. We've had help, some of us more than others, along the way — from others and, most importantly, from God. Without God giving us the ability and opportunity to earn money, it simply would not have happened.

Additionally, whatever money we have is not really ours to spend as we wish. Whether we have much or little, it's God's money. He is simply allowing us to earn, spend, and invest on his behalf.

Money LifeHack #3

It's not our money, but a gift to be used wisely.

STOP and THINK

1. How does knowing that money is a gift from God change your perspective on it?

2. Would you call yourself a good manager or steward of money? If so, how? If not, what is one action step you could take today to change that?

3. How can good stewardship of money affect your personal finances in the long run?

Chapter 4

MasterCard, I'm a Slave to You

I'm in debt. I am a true American.

— Balki Bartokomous (fictional character from late '80s/early '90s TV sitcom, Perfect Strangers)

How about this for coincidence? As I'm sitting down at my computer to edit the latest version of this chapter on debt, a website that is still on my computer screen from my last session is featuring an advertisement for the American Express Business Gold Rewards Card. The tagline for the ad is "Purchasing power that can grow as your business grows."

What's even more eye-catching is the fact that the technology used for the ad actually allowed the advertiser to use my headshot in the advertisement itself! They're using my profile picture for a social media website (LinkedIn) to personalize the ad just for me.

IT'S EVERYWHERE YOU WANT TO BE

This is just one example of the sophisticated marketing tactics credit card companies use. Through slogans like "It's everywhere you want to be," and card names like Gold, Platinum, or Elite, their messages appeal to our sense of adventure, desire for prestige, and our quest for happiness.

Of course, credit cards are just one part of the personal financial services we're offered by lending institutions. These companies also want to get our attention in order to sell us loan products for going to college, starting a business, buying a car, purchasing a home, or tiding us over until our next paycheck. They're more than eager to help us go into debt.

SIGN HERE

Our acceptance of consumer debt, including credit card, mortgage, and student loan debt, is a specter that casts a big shadow on the American Dream. As of December 2014, American consumers owed $11.74 trillion in debt, an increase of 3.3 percent from the previous year. This tally includes $882.6 billion in credit card debt, $8.14 trillion in mortgage debt, and $1.13 billion in student loans.

With the average American household's credit card debt standing at almost $16,000, mortgage debt at over $155,000 and student loan debt at over $32,000, I think we can agree that credit card and financial institution marketing is definitely working on us (NerdWallet).

THE TOLL

While financial institutions may benefit from us carrying debt, the real cost of borrowing money is taking a toll on us. Yes, borrowing costs us money, in the form of interest payments. However, this is not the whole story. Borrowing is costing us much more.

First of all, it's affecting our health. According to *Medical Daily's* 13 July 2014 article called "The Effects of Debt Reach Further Than Just Stress," the stress of debt raises our blood pressure, which results in 17 percent higher risk of hypertension and 15 percent risk of stroke. In addition, stress caused by debt can also result in insomnia, eating disorders, and other heath complications.

Second, our mental health can also be affected by the stress of debt. According to this same research, people in debt are three times more likely to suffer from mental health problems than people without debt. The mental problems also increase as debt increases. Studies have shown that depressive symptoms increase by 14 percent with each 10 percent increase in overall debt. These symptoms, if left to fester long enough, result in depression.

'TIL DEBT DO US PART

In addition to our mental and physical health, debt also puts a strain on our relationships. According to an October 23, 2009 *New York Times* article titled "Money Talks To Have Before Your Marriage," the odds of finances being the catalyst for divorce are 45 percent. In other words, almost half of all divorces are due to financial issues, with debt being the primary culprit.

The relationship casualties extend beyond marriage as well. Relationships between families, friends, and business partners are often negatively affected by financial debt.

THE AMERICAN DREAM

If you, like me, are in debt or have been in debt, none of what we just mentioned is surprising. We've been there. We've experienced the stress of debt. But why do we still do it? Why do we succumb?

Maybe we take on debt out of habit. We've always done it and know no other way. Maybe we don't see how we can live on what we earn; we borrow out of perceived necessity.

In my case, I borrowed money early in my adult life to purchase things like a used car and my first home. In the case of my first home, it just seemed to be the thing to do. How else was I to achieve the American Dream of owning a home?

WHAT'S YOUR SCORE?

Another reason many of us started down the path of debt is that we were encouraged to establish our credit by obtaining a credit card, car loan, or student loan. We were taught that we need a good credit score so that we can borrow more money to obtain what we need.

Even our government encourages us to "stimulate the economy" by spending (and often borrowing), irrespective of our financial condition and long-term goals. Programs like 2009's "Cash for Clunkers," which provided US residents economic incentives to trade in less fuel-efficient vehicles for a new, more fuel-efficient ones, lure us into making purchases by lowering interest rates or providing tax credits, among other tactics.

While reasons abound as to why so many of us are in debt, have you ever stopped to think what God has to say about debt?

IT'S A SIN?

Some may argue, but as far as I can tell, the Bible doesn't necessarily call debt a sin. If we go back to the parable of the talents in Matthew, mentioned in chapter 3, Jesus specifically mentions the value of earning interest on our money. If Jesus made it a point in the story to praise the servants who earned interest, it stands to reason that he is fine with at least some form of loaning and borrowing money, tied in to investing. We don't know how the servants made the money grow, in this example, but they obviously loaned the money to an entity who then used the capitol to make even more money, some of which trickled back down to the servants.

Another place where the Bible brings up debt, but doesn't necessarily say it's wrong is in the Old Testament book of

Exodus, chapter 22, verse 25. Yes, God does instruct the lender to not charge interest to a needy borrower, but he doesn't say it's a sin to be a borrower or lender. This same thought is echoed in Leviticus 25:36.

BORROWERS

The Bible also addresses those who owe money. Numbers 30:2 and Romans 13:8 both instruct us to be true to our word and pay our debts.

Note the message here is not necessarily that we shouldn't go into debt; there are situations where incurring debt may be the only way to overcome a temporary setback. The verses do state, however, that if we do incur debt, we should honor that commitment and pay up. Psalm 37:21 actually calls someone who does not repay what he owes "wicked."

YELLOW

Before we completely greenlight debt, however, let's look at some other verses that give us reason to be cautious about it. In Ecclesiastes 5:5, Solomon writes that it's better for us not to vow at all than to make a vow and not fulfill it.

Maybe you've never considered a swipe of that Visa card being considered a vow, but what we are really saying by charging a purchase or taking out a loan is that we agree to pay back the principle, in addition to any interest. It's a promise, based on the assumption that we will, in the future, be able to pay back this loan.

While our intentions may be good, the yellow caution flag must be raised here. Yes, we may not foresee having a problem paying back a bank or credit card. We may have the desire to pay back a debt, but we don't know what the future holds.

James 4:13–15 articulates this idea fairly well:

> *Now listen, you who say, "Today or tomorrow we will go to this or that city, spend a year there, carry on business and make money." Why, you do not even know what will happen tomorrow. What is your life? You are a mist that appears for a little while and then vanishes. Instead, you ought to say, "If it is the Lord's will, we will live and do this or that."*

The writer is warning us not to makes promises or vows that we may or may not be able to fulfill on our own.

I'M A SLAVE

Another way the Bible cautions us about debt is in the way it compares debt to slavery. Proverbs 22:7 actually calls the borrower a "slave to the lender." In other word, if we owe debt, we have proverbial shackles that tie us up. We seem to always have something hanging over our heads, so to speak.

The concept of being enslaved by debt is also echoed Deuteronomy 15:1 in which God instructs his people to cancel each other's debts at the end of the seventh year. By giving this guideline, he is acknowledging the burden that people carry when they are in debt.

I imagine it was also a disincentive for lenders. After all, if I knew that whatever money you borrowed from me would not have to be paid after the seventh year, I certainly would think twice about letting you borrow it.

TO BORROW OR NOT TO BORROW

Even though we can't definitely say that all debt is wrong, I think we would agree that God's ideal would be that we are not in debt. He acknowledges the possibility, but certainly doesn't want it to be a way of life for us.

Yes, we may borrow to invest in our business or to pay for a major unexpected life event, but borrowing should be the exception and not the rule. We need to think of it as a worst-case scenario instead of the easy way out.

Let's remember that debt has a way of slowly choking the life out of us. Incurring even a small amount of debt can take its toll our health, relationships, and overall quality of life.

HELP!

If you find yourself in unwanted debt, know that you're not alone. Many of us have been there and are continuing to climb out of debt we've incurred over the years.

Fortunately, good advice is available. There are many books, podcasts, websites, and other resources available to help. Some of you may even need some one-on-one counseling to help you create a plan to get out of debt. For a list of resources, please log on to gabrielaviles.com.

Money LifeHack #4

Borrow sparingly, if at all.

STOP and THINK

1. Do you believe it's possible to live free of debt?

2. If you were completely debt-free, how would that change your life?

3. Is there something you could do right now to begin to get out of debt?

Chapter 5

Endless Summer

Ants think winter all summer.

— *Author Unknown*

Although it took repeated viewings, prompted by my kids, I finally became a fan of the Disney movie phenomenon Frozen. If you haven't seen this animated musical, it's about Princess Anna venturing off to find her older sister, Elsa, who has inadvertently set off an "eternal winter" with her powers. Along this epic journey, we also meet several interesting characters — including everyone's favorite snowman, Olaf (no offense, Frosty).

In one of my favorite scenes, Olaf breaks out into a song called "In Summer," in which he dreams about what it would be like to enjoy a hot summer. He sings about dandelions, sipping cool drinks in the sand, getting gorgeously tanned, summer breezes, blue skies, and being surrounded by friends and fun. Of course, we all know what happens to snow in summer, but in spite of that minor detail, "In Summer" is the kind of song that can get anyone in that endless summer mood.

While there are places on the planet with extremely hot temperatures year-round, most of are not able to experience endless summers (unless you are the type who travels to warmer places in winter). Here in Tennessee, we are fortunate enough to have sun in the spring and fall as well, but eventually winter does hit us!

FINANCIAL FROST

The analogy of summer and winter holds true not only for weather, but also in our finances. Some of us have experienced a "financial summer," in which money, like sand and sunshine, was in abundance. We had secure jobs, bringing in enough to cover what we needed, as well as additional funds to enjoy. We were healthy and felt good about treating ourselves to dinners out, concert and sporting events, new outfits, vacations or new cars.

But then it hit us. We unexpectedly found ourselves in a financial frost. The car transmission malfunctioned. The hot water heater no longer heated our water. We had an emergency room visit.

Even worse, we lost our job — it's happened to me three times — and we were bleeding both on the expense and income side of things.

If this has never happened to you, don't worry. Life is bound to throw you a curveball at some point. Financial winters do come eventually!

PSR

I imagine most of us know instinctively to save. We've been taught about "rainy days" and emergencies. After all, a piggy bank is standard issue for most children.

So while there are those who don't save at all, most of us simply do not save enough. We feel good about saving a little bit, but are we really preparing ourselves for the unexpected?

Since 1959, the US Bureau of Economic Analysis has regularly published the PSR (Personal Savings Rate), defined as the ratio of household income saved versus household net disposable income. Since PSR tracking began, the record for personal savings was in May of 1975, reaching an all-time high of 14.6 percent. That meant that for every dollar made by the American workforce, 14.6 percent was put into savings. The record low was .8 percent in April of 2005, with the figures in 2014 being in the 5 percent range.

NO FUN

So why do we, as a nation, no longer save at the levels we used to? Reasons vary, of course, but I like to sum it up like this: saving is no fun! We work hard and then expect to be rewarded by buying things that we need or want — and buying them now. In fact, we often feel like we deserve these things after working so hard; at least I've felt that way at times.

Not only is saving money way less fun than spending it, but we tend to fall into the trap of feeling immune to major financial catastrophes. We don't expect to be the one to lose a job, have an unexpected medical emergency, or be the victim of a natural disaster. We can easily feel secure with our jobs, health, finances, and everything else around us. What could possibly go wrong?

Not that we should live in fear of financial ruin. The Bible is clear about us not living in fear. But is there a larger part that we need to play in preparing for the unexpected?

THE SLAMMER

In the book of Genesis, we are introduced to a man named Joseph who lived in Canaan. Joseph was one of twelve sons born to Jacob.

Although Joseph was a fine young man, he may have lacked a little in the humility department. Already not a favorite among his brothers because he was his dad's favorite (you might remember that his dad gave him the famous coat of many colors), Joseph continued to drive a wedge between himself and his brothers by sharing a dream with them that predicted they would bow down to him sometime in the future.

Due to his humility-challenged ways, his brothers conspired to get rid of him. To make a long story short, he ended up in Egypt as a slave, serving in the house of one of Egypt's high officials. Although he faithfully did his job, he was falsely accused of seducing his master's wife and ended up in jail.

DREAM WEAVER

But Joseph had something in his back pocket and God used it to spring him out of the slammer: a God-given ability to interpret dreams. Joseph accurately predicted that one cellmate's dream meant he would go free, and another cellmate's dream meant birds would eat the eyeballs out of his corpse.

And then, wouldn't you know it, Pharaoh himself started having dreams that no one could interpret. Enter Joseph, fresh out of jail. He explained to Pharaoh and everyone else in earshot that the dreams meant something critically important for Egypt's future: there would be seven years of bumper crops followed by seven years of famine.

So Pharaoh put Joseph in charge of a nationwide grain-storage effort. During the seven years of plenty, Joseph, now as second in command, collected large amounts of grain, "like the sand of the sea." Genesis tells us that he stored so much that they stopped keeping records of it; it was too much grain to quantify.

When the seven years of famine began, Joseph had stored enough to begin providing it back to his countrymen. Not only that, but he was able to also sell grain to other countries because the famine had affected the entire region.

The grain savings plan worked! All of Egypt, and even other nations, were saved due to Joseph's dream interpretations, civic management skills, and of course, Pharaoh's wisdom in saving for the future.

Had you been in Joseph's shoes, I'm guessing you would have done the same thing. It's kind of a no-brainer. When you know something terrible is going to happen, you, like any normal person, would certainly opt to do the same.

But the truth is, most of us don't have those dreams. Emergencies and even catastrophes remain unforeseen.

BEHOLD, THE ANT

In their behaviors ants display many notable qualities, including the way they collect food. Instinctively knowing that there is no such thing as an endless summer, they forage for food not only for the current season, but for the winter ahead.

Solomon even acknowledges their wisdom in Proverbs chapter 30. The ant is lauded for being of "little strength," yet storing up food in the summer.

OBJECTION, YOUR HONOR

I hope by now, if you're not already a saver, you're challenged to plan for those winter months. You realize that none of us knows what the future will bring, so a regular savings plan is a must.

Some of you, however, may still have your objections:

1. "I don't make enough money to save." While you may not make the kind of money you would like to (most of us are probably in that category), saving has nothing to do with income level and everything to do with attitude. If you are earning a paycheck, you can save. It may be a small amount, but you can begin to save up for an emergency fund right now.

2. "I like to use my credit card for emergencies." While credit cards can certainly help if you're in a pinch, this is not a long-term strategy for financial success. Having your own emergency fund instead of racking up credit card debt (or even borrowing from the bank) can save you hundreds, even thousands in interest payments, ultimately putting you ahead financially.

3. "I'll save when I get a little older." While young people tend to feel invincible, unfortunately winter

comes to them as well. Saving now can prevent you from a lifetime of trying to recover from a financial catastrophe. Plus, the sooner we begin saving, the sooner we can enjoy the benefits of compound interest.

PREMEDITATED SPENDING

One important tip that can help us carve out money for savings is to create a budget before we begin spending our paycheck. Yes, premeditated spending means thinking through the process up front so that we don't overspend and can still set aside some for a rainy day.

JUST SAY NO

Another tip to help us stick with our budget, to include savings, is being able to say, "no." Denying ourselves of that extra shot in our latte, that designer shirt, that fancy restaurant, or anything unnecessary that causes us to go over our budget is tough, but sticking to a budget with a built-in savings plan can definitely help us during those financial winters.

Money LifeHack #5

Let's store some for the winter!

STOP and THINK

1. Do you consider yourself a saver? Why or why not?

2. If you don't already have any emergency savings, how would you feel knowing that you have at least $1000 saved up in case of something unforeseen? If you do have some savings, do you feel like you have enough to hold you in case of a job loss or large medical emergency?

3. What is currently hindering you from saving more money? How can you tweak your budget in order to increase your savings? What are some habits that could change?

Chapter 6

Give It Away

Greedy little people in a sea of distress; keep your more to receive your less.

> *— from the song "Give It Away" by John Frusciante, Flea, and Anthony Kiedis, recorded by the Red Hot Chili Peppers*

If you were one of the 111.5 million people who watched Super Bowl XLVIII between the Seattle Seahawks and the Denver Broncos in February of 2014, you witnessed not only a big victory for Seattle, but also the half-time show featuring Bruno Mars and the Red Hot Chili Peppers.

As a fan of the Chili Peppers from my college days, I was giddy when they performed the song, "Give It Away." While music can mean different things to different people, to me, the song, still one of my all-time favorites, is a celebration of living a life of generosity and love.

$300+ BILLION

Along with the Red Hot Chili Peppers, it seems that many Americans have also discovered the benefits of giving. According to the Giving Institute's "Giving USA" 2014 report, charitable giving exceeded $335 billion in 2013, up from $316 billion 2012. Although down from its 2007 peak of $344 billion, the last few years have seen steady growth in donations to religious organizations, as well as groups that support education, human services, health, the environment, and various other nonprofits.

As for the donor pool, 72 percent of the giving came from individuals like us, with the balance coming from corporate giving, bequests or money donated upon someone's death, and foundations.

THE HOLDOUTS

While the statistics show that many do give, others of us hold back. Yes, we have that built-in desire to help people.

We want to feel good about contributing to good causes.. We want to give, but these nice thoughts don't always translate into action

The reasons for not giving are many. First of all, we don't see how we could possibly afford giving when we're barely paying our own bills. We fear that if we give, we won't have enough to cover our own needs.

Some of us may not give because we are stuck in analysis paralysis. With so many good causes out there, we can't seem to decide where to give.

Others of us who are barreling forward with eliminating debt, saving, investing, and building towards a financially secure future, can't get our heads around giving on a regular basis. It seems counterintuitive to give when we are determined to get our own house in order.

Finally, there are others of us who look to those appearing more fortunate than us to do the giving. Why should we be the ones to sacrifice when there are others, in our estimation, that can really afford to give?

While these concerns and ideas may have merit, let's explore what the Bible says about generosity and giving.

GLEANINGS

The principle of giving, specifically of giving to the needy, is foundational to the Bible. In the Old Testament, giving to the poor was part of the "Feast of Weeks," a celebration of the first fruits of the wheat harvest. Part of this important celebration included field owners leaving the edges of their field unharvested and allowing useful parts ("gleanings") to remain after harvesting so that the poor could take them.

In the New Testament, we also find the principle of giving to those in need. In Luke 3:11, John the Baptist tells a crowd to share their food and clothing with those who need them (technically, he says their "tunic" or coat), while in Acts 20:35, Paul also reminds us to help the impoverished and adds that it better to give than to receive.

Finally, in Matthew (22:37–40), Jesus also reminds us to love our neighbor as ourselves. In other words, if we wouldn't let ourselves go hungry, we shouldn't let our neighbors go without either.

SO YOU DIDN'T INVENT FACEBOOK

Sometimes we want to give, but are discouraged by the fact that we can't give much. After all, most of us are not Mark

Zuckerberg, cofounder of Facebook, who in 2013 donated almost $1 billion to one organization alone (Silicon Valley Community Foundation). We are "regular" people, working a nine-to-five, trying to make ends meet.

Once again, we can turn for guidance to the Old Testament Jewish feasts, mentioned in Deuteronomy 16:13–17. During these three feasts, including the Feast of Weeks previously mentioned, God asks the men to bring a gift, in proportion to the way that God had blessed them. In other words, even though he expected more from those that had more to give, the expectation was that everyone should contribute!

SMILE

In the New Testament, Paul encourages to give generously and with a smile. He tells us not give out of guilt or pressure, but out of our own desire. He adds that we should give without expectation (2 Corinthians 9:6–7).

THE BIG PAYBACK

While we don't give to the poor to get back, the Bible provides a pretty nice incentive. The big payback is that when we are in trouble, God will help us! Specifically, these verses state that God will protect us from our enemies; he will preserve our lives, and restore us to full health.

Solomon, the wisest man who ever lived (and King David's son), also gives us insight into the rewards for those who give to the poor:

> *One person gives freely, yet gains even more;*
> *another withholds unduly, but comes to poverty.*
> *A generous person will prosper; whoever refreshes*
> *others will be refreshed. (Proverbs 11:24–25)*

> *Whoever is kind to the poor lends to the Lord,*
> *and he will reward them for what they have done.*
> *(Proverbs 19:17)*

> *Those who give to the poor will lack nothing, but*
> *those who close their eyes to them receive many*
> *curses. (Proverbs 28:27)*

In the New Testament, Paul also adds that the generous will be made "rich in every way," (2 Corinthians 9:10).

THE GOLDEN RULE

I would be remiss if I didn't mention the good old Golden Rule, found in Matthew 7:12:

So in everything, do to others what you would have them do to you, for this sums up the Law and the Prophets.

While this verse doesn't list specific benefits to helping those in need, it does remind us that at some point, we have been or might be the ones in need.

Money LifeHack #6

Let's give (some of) it away.

STOP and THINK

1. How can being generous help you, even if your own financial situation is not where you'd like it to be?

2. Do you consider yourself a generous person? If so, why? If not, what's holding you back?

3. Are there organizations, causes, or people you believe in that could use your help financially?

Chapter 7

BREAK IT DOWN

"After all is said and done, more is said than done."

— *Anonymous*

We've now talked about six ways to *rethink* money. We've touched on money not buying happiness, money not being evil, and money being a gift for us to steward. We've also highlighted the beauty of living debt-free, saving, and giving.

Now let's put what we know into action (something many don't do!). My first recommendation would be to pray; ask God to help you set your personal finances in order. As we've learned, he is very interested in our personal finances and how we handle them. After all, he gives the ability to make wealth for a purpose.

Next, I would take a realistic look at your personal budget. If you don't already have a budget, well, that's your first step. If you do have a budget, review it. Break it down. Are you spending God's money wisely? Are you saving and giving like you should? Is there room for emergencies?

Many of us will have our work cut out just taking this step. It can easily become overwhelming to even *start* a budget. After all, most of us never really learned these life skills at school or at home.

That's OK. Cut yourself some slack and just start the process. Start by jotting down all of your current expenses by category (home, groceries, gas, bills, clothes, etc). You may have to do some guessing at first, but that's normal. Most of us don't know exactly what we pay for certain things until we take the time to keep track of it all.

As you start to write down what you're spending in various categories, over a period of time (maybe a few weeks and/ or months), you'll start to see a pattern of where your money is going. And you might be surprised to find out exactly how much you're spending on certain things. You might even discover places you can cut in order to funnel cash into other areas like paying off debt, saving, and giving.

Speaking of debts, you'll also want to write down all of your debts and begin to figure out how you can slowly (or maybe quickly ... depending on your situation), eliminate those. This might involve downgrading to a car that is paid for, selling some things, and/or cutting expenses to begin paying off those long overdue bills. Each situation will be different, but fortunately help can be found online, in books, through podcasts and radio shows and even through others you know who might be a step ahead.

My one encouragement is to not get discouraged. Do what you can now — and over time, things will change. It may take weeks, months, or even years, but the payoff will be worth it!

Also, rest assured that you're in good company. Most of us, at one time or another, have been in less than ideal financial predicaments, so you're not alone. It might take a little sweat and patience, but you can turn your situation around, regardless of your current status.

Thanks for taking this adventure with me. For some of you, this may have been a good reminder, but I hope that for others, this book has helped you to rethink your personal finances and, of course, take action!

For specific resources that will help you even further, please visit my website at gabrielaviles.com.

Chapter 8

LifeHack #1 – Extended Version (Bonus Chapter)

Let's start at the very beginning. A very good place to start.

— from the song "Do-Re-Mi" by Oscar Hammerstein II and Richard Rogers, recorded by Julie Andrews

If you have a favorite song, you'll know what I'm talking about. The joy in realizing that a song that moves you is not only available in the short, three- to four-minute radio version you first heard, but is also available in a much more satisfying, extended version. Maybe it's a longer live version or maybe it's more of an extended dance or club version. Either way, you're elated to be able to extend your listening pleasure.

Of course, if you don't care for a particular song, then hearing an extended version of it is probably not going to make your day. It might actually drive you crazy like it does me when it seems like the ChaCha Slide or the Electric Slide is seemingly going on forever during a wedding reception.

This chapter is kind of like that. Some of you may want to sit out, take a bathroom break, or go get some more wedding cake or punch. This extended ChaCha Slide is not for you. The financial portion of the book has concluded and you're ready to call it a night.

Others of you, however, will want to get back on the dance floor and continue the fun. For those of you in the latter category, here you go. Those of you in the former category, you've been warned.

HAPPINESS REVISTED

For those of you still with me, I'd like for us to revisit our first Money LifeHack: money does not equal happiness. While I'm a fan of all six LifeHacks I've outlined in this book, understanding and implementing the first LifeHack, in my opinion, can have the most impact on your life.

To recap, we learned that money affords us the basics of shelter, food, clothing, and other necessities and wants. Yes, it can even provide us with that new version of our favorite smart phone.

However, what happens when the next new and improved version of the smart phone comes out with the fancy new operating system and features? All of sudden, our once amazing smart phone doesn't seem so smart anymore. That same gadget that once brought us so much joy and pride now seems second rate. We might even start to rationalize why we really need to spend hundreds of dollars for the latest version (and why we need to be first in line for it).

I DON'T SKIP
THE COMMERCIALS

Even before working in advertising sales, I was drawn to highway billboards, print ads, radio jingles, and television commercials. I'm intrigued by trying to discern who the advertiser is targeting, why they used a certain graphic or image, what music bed they chose, what fonts were used, and whether it was successful in creating the desired call-to-action (at least in my opinion).

Now in the age of digital advertising, the geek in me continues to ponder ads I find on web sites, emails that come to my inbox, as well in video ads that run before those funny YouTube cat videos (not that I watch cat videos, but you know what I mean). Yes, I could easily ignore, delete, or skip those ads, but I'm too interested not to engage with them.

You don't have to pick apart advertisements like me to know that advertisers tap into our desire to find happiness by acquiring their products and services. In fact, many advertisers spend millions (even billions) every year to not only make us aware of their product's features and pricing, but to tap into that desire. Whether it's a new car, toothpaste, or a diet plan, advertisers play into our quest to find fulfillment and happiness in products and services available to us by simply laying down some cash.

WE ARE FAMILY

Some of us might say that the key to lifelong happiness is definitely not money, but relationships. Fulfillment can be found in loving and being loved. As a husband and dad,

I can definitely attest to the fact that loving my wife and kids and having them love me back is a fulfilling thing. There's nothing like having my children, Zoe, Evan, and Angelina hug me and call me Daddy.

You may feel the same about your spouse and kids. What a joy it is to also have parents, siblings, and other family members who love you no matter what, as well as friends who do the same.

However, because these loved ones are imperfect humans, and of course, the world is not perfect, these relationships may not always bring us lasting happiness. Sure, there might be good times, but then disappointments occur. Expectations go unfulfilled. Life happens. People change. Circumstances change. We change. All of these factors and more can result in relationships that no longer bring us the lasting happiness we once thought they might.

ON TOP OF THE WORLD

Others may argue that happiness and fulfillment are found in achieving success in entertainment, business, politics, athletics, or other endeavors that take us to the top in our field. We spend ourselves, sacrificing ourselves with the notion that once we reach our goal, we will be happy, fulfilled, and on top of the world, but is that really the case? Is that the answer to happiness? Actor and comedian Jim Carrey says it best: "I think everybody should get rich and famous and do everything they ever dreamed of so they can see that it's not the answer."

While money, relationships, fame, achievement, and other things can certainly make us smile and give us a temporary high, deep down, we know there's more. We know there has to be an answer to satisfy that longing inside all us.

THE CURE

At the risk of oversimplifying this quest for happiness (a topic that has been written about endlessly), I'm going to suggest that there is one sure way to happiness. Yes, I said it. There is one way to have more than just temporary smiles and highs. There is one way to live a life of happiness, irrespective of your circumstances.

No, I'm not saying that there is a way to avoid stress, pain, difficulties, broken relationships, health problems, financial issues, and the many things we all face. There's no one way to never have anything bad happen to us. After all, we're no longer in the Garden of Eden (before the fruit and snake incident).

What I am saying, however, is that through all of life's ups and downs, we can find happiness by *living with purpose*. Waking up every day, knowing that there is a reason for us to be alive and breathing, and going to bed feeling good about accomplishing a small portion of that brings a level of happiness that cannot be bought.

While this sounds good, most of us, truthfully, don't really know our purpose or even how to find it. We might have ideas, based on our interests, talents, assessments, or the opinion of others. However, we still find ourselves not knowing exactly why we're here on this planet.

Some, like the Dali Lama, would argue that "the purpose of our lives is to be happy." But is it really? Are we really able to obtain happiness by pursuing it?

THE DOCTOR

This is where we come back to God, the same one who can help us with our personal finances. While clues can be found in other places, the only way to truly understand our purpose is by having him define it. After all, he made us. He designed each one of us, specifically, to accomplish something specific. He handcrafted each one of us with a particular body shape, eye color, hair texture, personality, as well unique abilities and interests that are perfectly suited to fulfill whatever he has called us to do.

FRUSTRATION

Of course, frustration can kick in when we don't feel like we know what God is saying about our purpose. We might read the Bible, pray, and talk to others we deem more spiritual than us, but still feel in the dark. If that's you, don't worry. God is not out to frustrate you. He may choose to tell you what you were made to do right away or he may opt to reveal it along life's journey. Either way, you can trust him to follow through when you ask him to help you.

The good news is that even when we don't have any clarity, we can still live on purpose, trusting in God, who has our back. We can wake up knowing that even if we don't know the full details, as we ask him for wisdom to live our lives on a daily basis, he will guide us along the way. We take one day at a time, trusting that more will be revealed as we need it.

Are you ready for true happiness ... the happiness that money can't buy? Are you ready to live with purpose? Are you ready to ask the Man Upstairs to help you live life full blast, as he intended you to live it?

NOTES

Chapter 1

Gross National Happiness

The Easterlin studiescan be found here:
http://graphics8. nytimes.com/images/2008/04/16/business/ Easterlin1974.pdf
— and here *http://www. pnas. org/content/107/52/22463.*

The Stevenson/Wolfers study can be found here:
http://www.nber.org/papers/w14282.

Chapter 3

Word of the Day

This definition is from the Merriam-Webster Collegiate Dictionary online:
http://www. merriam-webster. com/dictionary/steward

Chapter 4

'Til Debt Do Us Part
New York Times article ...

American Dream
This article from NerdWallet is available here:
http://www. nerdwallet. com/blog/credit-card-data/
average-credit-card-debt-household/
Information on our national debt can be found here:
http://www.usdebtclock.org/

Chapter 5

PSR
The data on the US PSR is available here: *http://www.*
tradingeconomics.com/united-states/personal-savings.

ACKNOWLEDGMENTS

"It takes a village" to write a book and now, it's time to thank some of the villagers:

First of all, a big thank you to my editor Jamie Chavez (jamiechavez.com), designer Randy Paulk (underthebigtop. com), research assistant, Dan Kassis (fencepostblog.com), as well as Jon Walker (gracecreates.com), who gave me much to chew on early in the process.

Thank you also to many others who have contributed time, encouragement, advice, feedback, resources, and prayer — including Mike Adams, Pastor Lyndon Allen, Terry Anderson, Mavette Augustine, Ana Aviles, Ciro Aviles, Esther Aviles, Todd Baker, Candace Blackstock, Rodney Bowen, Neil Brennan, Jeff Brown, Janene Burdick, Sam Butler, Jeff Cadavero, Mitch Canter, John Cantu, Jack Center, Jessica Chappell, Jerry Charles, Stan Chiang, Brian Church, Elizabeth Cobos, Ben Cooper, Biju & Nisha Daniel, Vinay Daswani, Tammy Daughtry, Julienne DesJardins, Jennifer Deshler, Jeremy Dunn, Jevonnah Ellison, Chris Erlanson, David Estes, Joanna Evans, Joel and Elizabeth

Evans, Josie Evans, Michael and Patricia Evans, Clark Gaither, Greg Glass, Anita Gonzalez, Jeremi Griggs, Ash Greyson, Ronei Harden, Austin Harrison, Drew Hart, Rob Harvey, Selena Headley, Lori Hensley, Julie Hyde, Kyle Johnson, Wendy Jones, Lucy Diaz Kurz, Erik Larsen, Anthony Lassiter, Pastor James Lowe, Joshua Lutz, Wayne Martin, Lynn McCain, John McKee, Dan Miller, Cheryl Goolsby Moats, Betty Mostella, Michelle Nipp, Eric Nordhoff, Linda Paek, Tom Perrault, Miriam Porter, Deborah Evans Price, Mike Priebe, Jim and Tami Rickwa, Toni Rigsby, Clinton Robertson, Karin Lopez Sandiford, Matt Scherr, Dave Schroeder, Victor and Annette Segura, Tonya Sparks, Tina Stephens, Toni Sterling, Will Stoup, Curtis Swartzentruber, Melissa Thomas, Michael Tyler, Rick Welke, Chris and Erica Well, Scott and Nila Whelan, and DeEtta West.

A special thanks to my friends at Trevecca University's Futuro Club, for being part of my focus group (especially Tatyana Collins, Roxanne Estrada, Katerine Hernandez, Quinyatta Jones, Aaron Sura), as well as members of my various support groups out there like Life FullBlast Insiders, SPI Franklin, Jon Acuff's Dreamers & Builders, and my 48 Days' Coaching With Excellence crew.

Thanks also to Jon Acuff, Jeff Brown, John Lee Dumas, Pat Flynn, Seth Godin, Dan Miller, and Dave Ramsey for continually inspiring me through your podcasts, blogs, and books!

Thank you to my wife, Tanya, who has believed in this idea for years and has supported me every step of the way.

Finally, thank you to God for the idea to write this book series back in 2000 and the resources to make it happen!

ABOUT THE AUTHOR

Gabriel Aviles is the author of Money LifeHacks: A 60-Minute Beginner's Guide to Rethinking Your Personal Finances, the first book in the Man Upstairs LifeHacks series. Born in Chile, he moved to New York City with his family at the age of five, before ultimately settling in Tennessee.

Gabriel has worked in the entertainment and media industry for over twenty years and is now expanding his influence as an author and coach. Aviles has earned his Dave Ramsey's Financial Coach Master Series certification and is also working toward completion of the 48 Days Coaching Mastery program with New York Times best-selling author Dan Miller.

He has completed two years of biblical training at Every Nation Leadership Institute in Nashville, Tennessee, has been a men's and marriage Bible study leader, and has also served in various other leadership roles within his local church including facilitator of Financial Peace University.

Married for more than a decade and proud father of three small children, Gabriel enjoys learning, traveling, playing Monopoly with his kids, watching Seinfeld reruns, and helping others live the life they were created to live. He also has what some would call a supernatural ability to "Name That Tune" in three notes or less.

For booking, coaching, or other inquiries, log onto www.gabrielaviles.com.